For the kindergarten teachers of Reiche School

First Edition   5 6 7 8 9 10

Library of Congress Cataloging in Publication Data
McMillan, Bruce.   Super, super, superwords.
Summary: Adjectives are used visually and grammatically to demonstrate the three degrees of comparison:
positive, comparative, and superlative.   1. English language—Comparison—Juvenile literature. 2. Vocabulary—
Juvenile literature. [1. English language—Comparison. 2. Vocabulary] I. Title.
PE1241.M36   1989   372.6′1   88-9342
ISBN 0-688-08098-7   ISBN 0-688-08099-5 (lib. bdg.)

SUPER
SUPER
SUPERWORDS

by BRUCE McMILLAN

Lothrop, Lee & Shepard Books   New York

HEAVY

HEAVIER

HEAVIEST

LOW

LOWER

LOWEST

SMALL

SMALLER

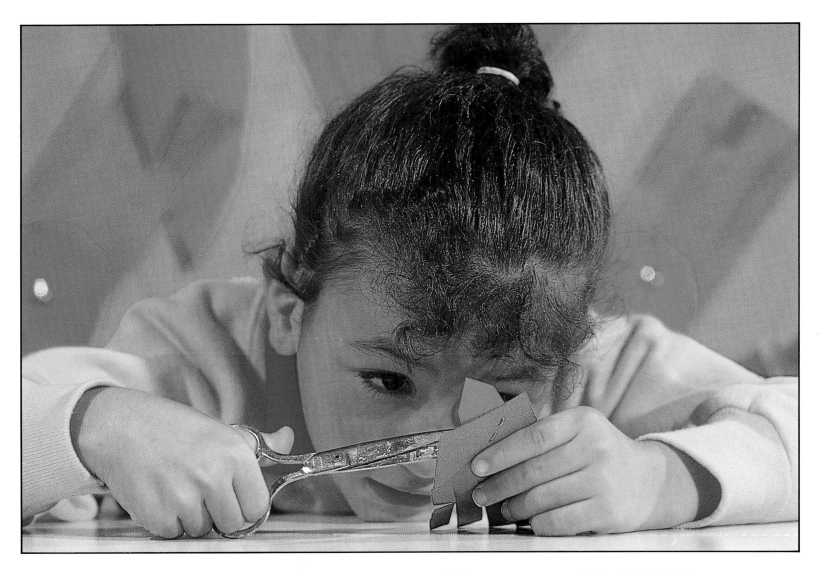

SMALLEST

YELLOW

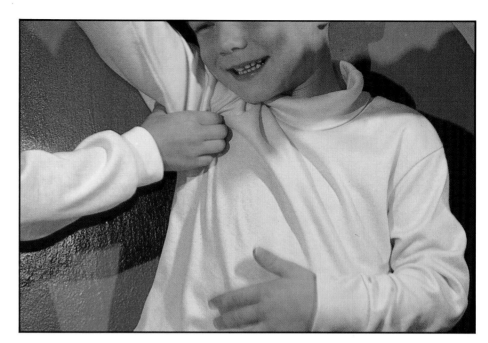

YELLOWER

YELLOWEST

TALL

TALLER

TALLEST

FULL

FULLER

FULLEST

SHORT

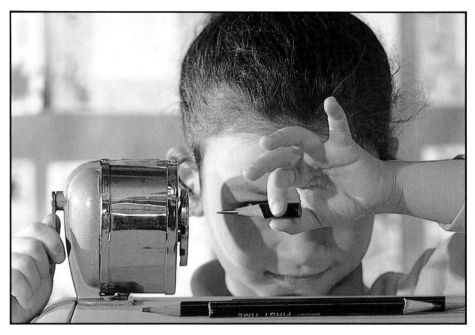

SHORTER

SHORTEST

FEW

FEWER

FEWEST

LONG

LONGER

LONGEST

BIG

BIGGER

BIGGEST

HIGH

HIGHER

HIGHEST

CLOSE

CLOSER

CLOSEST

LOUD

LOUDER

LOUDEST

THE END

ABOUT THIS BOOK

Super, Super, Superwords is the story of a child's kindergarten day. It is also a visual grammar lesson, introducing the concept of degrees of comparison and a basic way of expressing this concept verbally.

Words and photographs on each two-page spread demonstrate one adjective in its three degrees of comparison:

Positive ("tall") provides the initial reference.

Comparative ("taller") relates two persons, objects, or ideas, showing an increase in the quality expressed by the adjective.

Superlative ("tallest") shows a comparison among three or more; it expresses the extreme or unsurpassed extent of the quality.

Superwords can be used as an introductory lesson on vocabulary development, word usage, and word building. Adding the endings -er and -est to adjectives is the simplest way of forming comparatives and superlatives and is used throughout this book. At the next level of comparison development, the modifying words "more" and "most" are combined with longer adjectives, and then actual word changes like "good, better, best" can be mastered. *Superwords* is only the beginning.

The photographs were taken in the kindergarten classes at the Howard C. Reiche Community School in Portland, ME, with the full cooperation of principal Miriam Remar, the teachers, and the staff. All of the children photographed are students at Reiche School. Special thanks go to my new friend Leonór Rodriguez, for wearing the same clean outfit to school on so many days, and to our buddies (in order of appearance): Michael Barker, Timothy Hayward, Anthony Rosa, Jenny Ping Seavey, Jimmy Shaw, Amber Hanson, Bory Sem, Rollen Chom, Sok San Keo Pao, Matthew Blake, O'Neil Dameion Lindsay, and Kyle Whisler. We had a lot of fun at school.

The photographic lighting used indoors was a combination of three synchronized portable flash units (one a bare bulb) to provide the primary light, with an additional quartz light to warm the colors. The outside lighting was afternoon autumn sunlight, with the colors enhanced by a polarizing filter. A tripod-mounted motordriven Nikon FE2 camera was used with a 50, 105, or 200mm Nikkor lens. The film used was Kodachrome 64 processed by Kodak.